This book is dedicated with to my parents, Randy and John Morgan, for my fairytale childhood and for teaching me to always believe in magic. I love you more than the sun loves the moon!

A witch is a person who believes that all things are magical. They love animals, trees, flowers, bugs, rocks, crystals, the sun, the moon, and the earth.

They especially love other people. Witches know that they can do anything if they believe in themselves. Anyone can be a witch!

Witches like to connect with nature.

Witches work with the elements of water, air, fire, and earth in their spells.

Meditate with the Elements

To connect with the elements, find a quiet place to sit outside.

Touch the ground with your hands and feel how strong it is. This is the energy of Earth.

Feel the wind blow in your hair. Feel how soft and gentle it is. This is the energy of Air.

Feel the warm sun on your face. This is the energy of Fire.

Take a cool sip of water. All things need water to live. This is the energy of Water.

Imagine the feeling of all the elements moving into your heart or belly until you are calm and happy.

Draw a picture or write a
poem about how the
elements made you feel!

Create an Altar

Witches like having a special place in their room to meditate and do spells. It is a place they feel happy and strong.

You can make your own altar at home by creating a place for special items that make you feel magical.

Items for a Witch's Altar:

- Water
- Feathers
- Rocks
- Crystals
- Candles
- Acorns
- Flowers
- Anything you want!

Sweet Dreams Spell

Even witches have bad dreams sometimes. This spell can help make your dreams happy and magical.

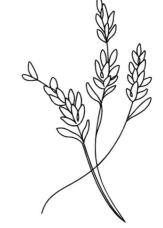

What you need:

- A small pouch or jar
- Dried Lavender flowers
- Chamomile flowers - the contents of a tea bag work fine!
- An amethyst crystal

Place all of the ingredients inside the pouch or jar, and then place it under your bed, pillow, or on your nightstand for sweet dreams!

Witches look for signs and symbols in nature. The butterfly is a symbol of fresh starts and happy changes. What changes would you like to make? Color the butterfly while imagining them.

Make Your Own Magic Wand

A wand is a tool that witches use to focus energy when they do spells. You can make your own!

What you need:
- A wooden stick from outside
- Paint

Once you have found your perfect wand wood, decorate it with colors and symbols that you love. You might paint pictures of magic symbols like hearts or stars on your magic wand. It's up to you to create what you want!

Bake Good Luck Cookies

Even witches need a little luck sometimes. Cinnamon helps attract good energy and luck. You can bake these cookies before a big test or anytime you need a boost of confidence!

Ingredients
- 2 cups of flour
- 3/4 cup and 1 tablespoon butter
- 1/2 cup of sugar
- 2 teaspoons of cinnamon

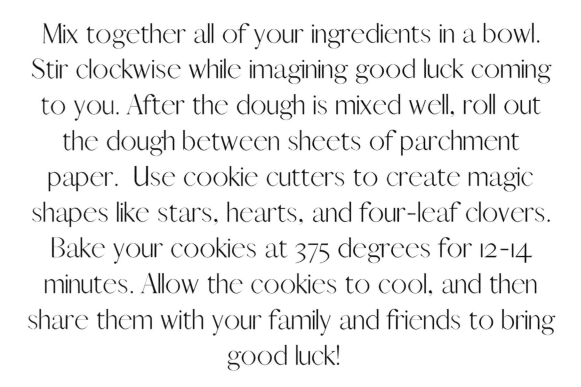

Mix together all of your ingredients in a bowl. Stir clockwise while imagining good luck coming to you. After the dough is mixed well, roll out the dough between sheets of parchment paper. Use cookie cutters to create magic shapes like stars, hearts, and four-leaf clovers. Bake your cookies at 375 degrees for 12-14 minutes. Allow the cookies to cool, and then share them with your family and friends to bring good luck!

Blessings for the Birds

Witches love all creatures, big and small. As the seasons change and it grows colder, it can be harder for birds to find food. You can bless the birds by creating natural bird feeders around your home.

What You Need
- Pinecones
- Peanut Butter
- Bird seed
- String or twine

Collect pinecones that have fallen off the trees and then tie a string to the top. Cover the pinecones with peanut butter and dip them in birdseed. Hang the blessings in the trees around your home or neighborhood to offer a helpful treat for the birds and squirrels.

Write Your Own Spell

Words are powerful! Witches use words to help make things happen. You can create a spell with words that rhyme, like a small poem. It can be very simple. For example:

With these words I say,
Today will be a good day.
Come what may!

Try out writing your own spell or poem!

_____

_____

_____

_____

_____

_____

Make Full Moon Water

The Full Moon is a special time for witches. It represents change and starting new. When the moon is full it has a powerful energy. Making full moon water can help you connect with the magic of the moon!

What You Need
- A clear jar or bottle
- Water

Fill your jar with water and then place it outside on the night of the full moon, where it can absorb the moonlight. Make sure you wake up early to go get your jar and bring it inside! You can use your full moon water in potions, or sprinkle it around your room to bring good energy!

Happy Hot Chocolate Potion

A cup of warm hot chocolate puts witches in the best mood! If you're feeling down in the dumps, make a tasty potion of Happy Hot Chocolate!

Ingredients

- 2 cups of your favorite milk
- 2 tbs of Cacao
- 1 tbs of honey or maple syrup
- 1/2 tsp of vanilla
- a pinch of cinnamon

Ask a grown-up to help you mix the ingredients together and warm them over the stove. Drink and enjoy with a friend!

Bubble Spell to Release Emotions

Witches have a lot of emotions, and sometimes they can get overwhelming. If you have some hard feelings that you want to let go of, try this bubble spell!

What You Need
- Bubbles

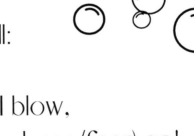

Repeat this spell:

With this bubble that I blow,
I let my (say the feeling: anger/sadness/fear) go!

Then, blow the bubble and imagine the feeling leaving your body with your breath and moving into the bubble. Watch the bubble until it pops, and know that your feelings have been released.

Knot Magic for Friendship

Bind your friendship together so that it lasts forever!
You can make a friendship bracelet using knots and give
it to your friends to help make your friendship even
stronger!

What You Need
- Embroidery floss in different colors
- Beads (optional)

Choose at least three different colors of embroidery floss
that remind you of your friend. You can make multiple
bracelets and use different colors for each friend. Get
creative and braid, knot, or weave the twine together. Feel
free to add beads or crystals along the way!

When you and your friends trade bracelets, say the following
spell as you knot them on:

We are tied together,
In Friendship forever!

Use these pages to:
create your own spells,
draw pictures,
or journal!

Printed in Great Britain
by Amazon